Hockeytown Hero™: The Steve Yzerman Story

An authorized biography

by

Shelley Lazarus

Cover design by Jeffrey Wisniewski

Proctor Publications, LLC • Ann Arbor • Michigan • USA

Library of Congress Catalog Number: 2001-131134

Publisher's Cataloging-in-Publication
(Provided by Quality Books, Inc.)

Lazarus, Shelley.
    Hockeytown hero : the Steve Yzerman story / by
Shelley Lazarus. -- 1st. ed.
    p. cm.
    Includes bibliographical references and index.
    ISBN: 1-928623-04-2

    1. Yzerman, Steve. 2. Hockey players--Canada--
Biography.   I. Title.

GV848.5.Y94L39 2001   796.962'092
                        QBI01-200084

www.otterbooks.net

ii

This book is dedicated to:

Dad,
who taught me to write a business letter

Janie,
who taught me the game of hockey

and

Eric,
who gives me time and support.

Acknowledgments

This book would not have been possible without the help of many people.

First I want to thank Steve. He was generous with his time and was cooperative throughout the project. It's a pleasure to be associated with such a talented, gracious, and humble person.

Darren Pang, Dick Todd, Herb Warr, Cathie Webster, Tim Carmichael, Rick Bugnet, and Peter Peckett were all extremely helpful when I was working on the Nepean and Peterborough chapters of the book. They provided names, numbers, stats and quotes when I needed them most.

I now have a greater appreciation for hockey beat writers for the *Detroit Free Press*, *The Detroit News* and *The Oakland Press*. The game story chronology built by reporters like Viv Bernstein, Nicholas J. Cotsonika, Keith Gave, Ansar Kahn, Jason La Canfora, Cynthia Lambert, John Lowe, Bill McGraw, Drew Sharp, Helene St. James, and Charlie Vincent enabled me to accurately rebuild Steve's career from the moment he set foot in Detroit to the present. Their stories also brought back lots of memories for me as I did my research. Special thanks to Lynn Henning, Charles Robinson, Ted Kulfan, and Paula Pasche who helped me at practice.

I also wish to thank the Detroit Red Wings organization for their help. Jimmy Devellano, John Hahn, Mike Kuta, Scotty Bowman, Dave Lewis, Barry Smith, John Wharton and a number of Wings players were generous with their time and patient with my questions. Bill Jamieson, former Public Relations Director for the Wings, was also helpful and shared many great stories.

A special thank you to Bryan Trottier. Your comments exemplify the respect and admiration people in and out of hockey have for Steve, both on and off the ice.

Gene Myers, Mary Schroeder, Gina Brintley, Owen Davis, and Jenny Koss of the *Detroit Free Press* were exceptionally helpful with the photos. Ron and Jean Yzerman provided the photos of Steve when he was young.

Thanks to Denise, Janie, Brad Betker, Jo-Ann

Barnas and members of my writing group who read the manuscript and offered comments and suggestions.

I want to recognize Stewart Roberts and Phil Stamp of *The A to Z Encyclopedia of Ice Hockey* (see Resources) who let me use many of their definitions in the glossary. Laura Ramus was helpful with the medical definitions.

Finally, I want to thank the students of Pine Lake Elementary School. You had some great questions!

Table of Contents

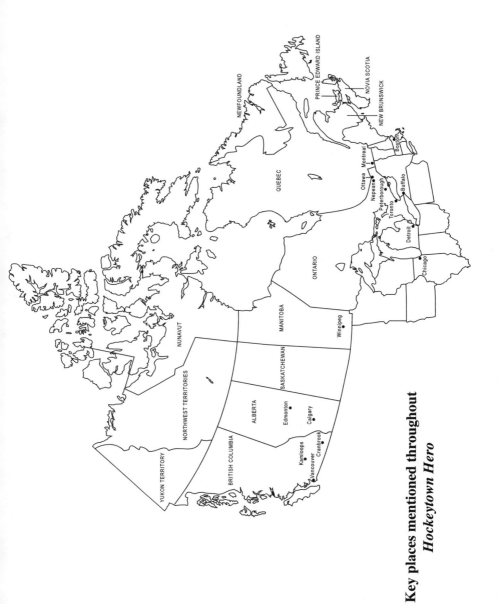

Key places mentioned throughout
Hockeytown Hero

The Stanley Cup. It had eluded Steve Yzerman for 13 years and the city of Detroit for 42. In 1997, all that changed. Now, for the second year in a row, Yzerman circled the ice, lifting hockey's prized possession high over his head. The Detroit Red Wings had just defeated the Washington Capitals 4-1, sweeping the series in four games as they had done the previous season against the Philadelphia Flyers. Moments earlier, Yzerman had raised the Conn Smythe Trophy recognizing him as the playoffs' Most Valuable Player. It was a night when Steve Yzerman finally got the credit and respect he deserved. It was a night every young, hockey-playing Canadian boy dreams of . . .

1

Everything Sports-Related

On a cold winter's day, Steve Yzerman, his older brother, Mike, and their parents headed to a frozen lake for a day of skating. Steve was about 3 years old and ready to take to the ice in a pair of **bobskates**. Although it would be another two years before he played organized hockey, it was the first step toward learning the skills that would make him a hockey superstar.

Steve was born to Ron and Jean Yzerman, May 9, 1965, in Cranbrook, British Columbia. As a young boy, Steve skated and watched a lot of hockey with his father. He remembers seeing the New York Rangers take on the Boston Bruins in one of the first professional hockey games they watched together on television. As Steve grew older, he began watching the Vancouver Canucks' games. The more he watched, the more he knew he wanted to play hockey.

Around this time, Mike started playing on an organized hockey team. After attending some of Mike's games, Steve asked his father if he could play too. Ron Yzerman told his son that, at age 4, he wasn't old enough yet. The following year, his father declared Steve was ready. Steve joined his first team and attended a hockey camp.

"I played as a 5-year-old but I couldn't skate," Steve says. "I could get up and fall down. Then I went to hockey camp that summer. That's where I learned how to skate and picked it up pretty quickly.

"My first year we played on a rink and they divided it into three. You played half across the ice. You had one game going in the end zone, one in the middle and one in the other end. We were 5-year-olds. We really couldn't stand up. That was great!"

His first goal was really nothing to be proud of.

"I had fallen down in front of the net," Steve told Bill McGraw, a *Detroit Free Press* reporter. "Their guy banked it off one of their guys' skates and into the net. I was lying there and I got credit for it."

Like most Canadian boys, Steve watched hockey, played on hockey teams, and dreamed of becoming a professional hockey player. He emulated his own hockey hero, the New York Islanders' Bryan Trottier. He admired the way Trottier conducted himself on the ice and saw him as a solid, all-around player. Steve also strived to be a great all-around player, imitating Trottier's every move, from the taping of his stick to the way he celebrated a goal.

But Steve didn't limit himself to hockey. He enjoyed a variety of sports and played them any time he got the chance. He sought out a neighborhood game as quickly as he did an organized match.

"I was into all sports," Steve says. "In the summer, we played hockey. We played street hockey. We played grass hockey. As a kid, it was sports and whatever game was going on, we were playing it."

Being such an avid sports fan, Steve did more than just watch and play. He admits sports were involved in every facet of his life. When Steve picked up a book, it was almost always one about a favorite athlete.

"I used to read biographies," Steve says. "I read about Bobby Orr. I read about Joe Namath, Fran Tarkenton and Kareem Abdul-Jabbar. Pretty much everything I did was sports-related."

But not all his sports-related activities were so serious. Steve and his brothers were also hockey card collectors. However, these cards didn't get the special treatment many collectors give their cards today.

"Yeah, we collected cards," says Steve, thinking back. "I had three brothers, so the four of us had stacks and stacks of them. What we used to do is play a game where you'd line them up on the wall, then flick them and try to knock over the other cards. That's what we did with them! We would all collect them, keep cards of all the players, and look at them. But we played games with them. When we were teenagers and we were all starting to move out of the house, we probably had a fortune's worth of old hockey cards, but my mom just threw them out. Collecting wasn't the big deal it is now."

Steve lived in Cranbrook until he was 7 years old. Living in another part of British Columbia for a couple of years, Steve took advantage of the rugged land that surrounded him. He expanded his sports repertoire to include hiking.

In 1973, when Steve was 8, he played for the Moose Pup All-Stars in Kamloops, British Columbia. This was one of his first travel teams. Steve's brother Mike also played for the team. Steve is in the front row, third from the right and Mike is next to him, second from right.

"We lived in a city called Kamloops for two years," he recalls. "It was a fun place to play. We lived on a street that was kind of the last street in the town and behind us were the hills. All summer, we spent our whole day hiking up in those hills. You could literally go forever. That was a fun place to live because there were a lot of outdoor things to do. When I played in Kamloops, actually, [hockey] became more competitive and we traveled around to local cities. As a 10-year-old, we moved to Ottawa and that's where I started playing soccer in the summer."

Although he had the company of his brothers and sister, he was also glad he played sports. It kept him busy and it helped him make friends in his new hometown.

"That definitely made it a lot easier," says Steve. "It was the easiest way to meet other kids and make friends. Playing on the hockey team kept me busy after school."

It was in Nepean, a suburb of Ottawa, Ontario, that Steve's hockey playing steadily increased. He was no longer playing in the **house leagues**.

"There are different levels," Steve says. "There's A, B and C and a lot of kids play. The A league, you do a lot more traveling. The B team is kids who didn't make the A team. Then after that it would basically just be local leagues, just in the area. They don't have to travel all over."

Steve had reached the level of play required to earn a position on a travel team. He was on the ice for practices and games as many as five days a week. He participated in tournaments. At 14, Steve was playing Junior A Tier 2 hockey in the Central Junior Hockey League (**CJHL**) with the Nepean Raiders. His parents, supportive of his hockey playing, took Steve wherever he needed to go.

In 1977, Steve's Pee Wee team won the Ontario Provincial Championship. Steve is in the front row, third from the right.

"My brother and I played a lot of hockey and my parents were constantly driving us around," Steve says. "We both played in a lot of tournaments where, from Ottawa, we'd drive to Toronto, all over Ontario, into Quebec, and occasionally down into the States. It was a big commitment for my parents and a real sacrifice for my sister and my two younger brothers. My parents were spending a lot of time during the hockey season with us."

Some of Steve's best memories of playing hockey as a youth come from his days in Nepean. When he played peewee hockey at age 12, Steve's team won the Ontario Provincial Championship. Later, when playing for the Raiders in 1980-81, Steve had one of his most memorable seasons.

"I played in that league as a 15-year-old and it was one of my most enjoyable years," Steve says. "We had a good team. That's when I became friends with Darren Pang. I played with a really good bunch of guys. I was 15 and playing with guys up to 20 years old. It was one of the most enjoyable years I'd had in hockey."

Steve contributed 38 goals and 54 assists to help the Raiders finish first in the regular season. Although Steve added four goals and 11 assists in the playoffs, the Raiders lost to the Gloucester Rangers in the finals. Steve left the league banquet with two trophies, Rookie of the Year and Outstanding Midget in the League, and the honor of being named the league's first-team All-Star center.

Pang remembers that, even at 15, Steve had incredible talent.

"It was very obvious," says Pang, a former goalie and now an announcer for ESPN. "Not only the fact that he was a real special individual player, I always thought that he was light years ahead of everybody else in terms of maturity. He always kind of kept himself on a nice even keel and then, when he got onto the ice, he did such special things with the puck."

He also remembers how Steve could spark the team.

"Whenever you were down a goal and you needed something special to happen," says Pang "he would literally put the team on his back and make something happen. You know, players like that, when they come around and you get a chance to play with them... I mean... nothing's for sure in life but you look and say, 'Oh boy, this guy's going to be a good one, if not a great one.' He's turned out to be a great one."

It was during this time that Steve began to think he might have a future playing hockey. When Steve was 14, the Raiders put him on a **protected list**, just like those used in the National Hockey League (**NHL**) drafts. This meant no other team could draft Steve to play for it. He was assured a spot on the Raiders' roster the following season.

"I started taking it seriously," Steve says. "That's when the junior team scouts started coming to watch the games."

In two years, Steve would find out how serious the scouts really were.

2

The Peterborough Years

At 16, most kids are in the middle of high school. They are hanging out with their friends, doing their homework and always have home as a haven. But this age brought a much different life for Steve. He moved up to Major Junior Hockey, drafted by the Peterborough Petes of the Ontario Hockey League. With 160 miles between Nepean and Peterborough, Steve had to make a move. In order to play for the Petes, he and teammate Mike Posavad would leave home and take up residence with Vince and Lottie Garvey. The Garveys lived two blocks from the arena and provided accommodations for a number of Peterborough players through the years. Steve remembers them fondly.

"A majority of the junior teams are supported really well through the community," says Steve. "Families volunteer to take in players. The team pays room and board. I was with an unbelievable family. They were an older couple. Their children were grown and they were big hockey fans. The Garveys were great people. [They] spoiled us rotten!"

Peterborough drafted Steve, impressed with the offensive ability he demonstrated in Nepean. Early in his career with the Petes, other strengths in his game emerged. Former Petes coach Dick Todd recalls that Steve didn't have many glaring weaknesses, even at 16.

At 16, Steve was drafted by the Peterborough Petes of the Ontario Hockey League.

"Steve came to us very young and very small, but he had tremendous offensive skills," remembers Todd. "Coming in to Peterborough, he was already very offensive-minded. If anything, we didn't have the toughness on the team to protect him. But Steve also had the ability to learn. He became a well-rounded player."

Todd also remembers Steve's unselfishness when it came to helping teammates score. One of the Petes' leading scorers was Bob Errey. One reason for that was Steve's play.

"Another thing Steve could do was draw the defense to him and pass off to Bob," Todd says. "Steve did all right when it came to scoring goals. He had between 40 and 50 his second year. But Bob's production was higher because Steve was able to get him open."

While playing for the Petes, team members were also required to attend school or work at a job. Expectations for players off the ice were just as high as when they were playing. Parents received progress reports monthly. If players were having difficulty with school, the team provided tutors. Steve attended Thomas A. Stewart Collegiate his two years in Peterborough. Todd remembers Steve handled school with the same confidence and finesse as hockey.

Todd, now a scout with the New York Rangers, was a medical and equipment trainer with the Petes when Steve started in 1981-82. Dave Dryden was head coach. That December, when team members had differences with Dryden's coaching style, Dryden left. Todd took over as head coach. He coached the remainder of Steve's two-year career with the Petes. Steve credits Dryden and Todd with teaching him important aspects of his game.

"It was beneficial for me," Steve says, "because it was a team where the two coaches that I played for spent a lot of time teaching me how to play away from the puck, meaning playing your position defensively. That was the first time I'd ever spent time, in practice or talking before the games, playing defensively. [They taught us] who to pick up **back-checking** and, in your own zone, what your responsibility was. Before that, when you practiced and played, you basically tried to make a play to score a goal. You didn't really work on the defensive part of the game. Going there was the first time

I spent any time on it. They stressed it there."

To this day, Todd remains one of Steve's favorite and most influential coaches.

"I really enjoyed playing for Dick Todd," says Steve. "He taught you a lot about the game and he was a really honest man. He'd tell you about the way you played. If he didn't like what you were doing or he was saying something to help you, he would just say it honestly, plain as day. Whatever it was, he wouldn't pull any punches. I really liked him for that. I was comfortable around him."

Todd, unlike other junior coaches, was known for playing all four lines consistently every game. He didn't give star players large amounts of ice time. Some coaches and players criticized this. They felt this philosophy hurt players' statistics and didn't allow standout players a chance to be recognized by pro scouts. However, Todd saw it differently. He felt this system gave every player a chance to contribute to the team's success. It also meant he wasn't rebuilding the team each year when he lost graduating players.

This system gave Steve somewhat average statistics for his two years in Peterborough. It also gave him something much more valuable: the concept that if he would play offense and defense with equal energy, the team could achieve larger goals. That would later enable Steve to adapt to coach Scotty Bowman's style in Detroit. Peterborough also gave Steve another opportunity that enhanced his hockey career: international competition.

"We had a pretty good team, but both years we lost in the second round of the playoffs," Steve remembers. "I learned a lot from playing there. I got to play in the World Junior Championships my second year in Peterborough, over in the Soviet Union. It was a great experience. We got the bronze medal."

When Steve left Peterborough, he knew he had a strong rating for the 1983 **NHL Entry Draft**. His second year at Peterborough, Steve's statistics were solid: 42 goals and 49 assists for a total of 91 points. He carved out a role as a play-making center with strong goal-scoring skills. He played under a coach whose philosophy focused on team effort and playing both ends of the rink. All this experience came together to make one nice package for some lucky NHL team. The question was: which one?

3

The Winged Wheel

Montreal was the site of the 1983 NHL Entry Draft. Steve was rated by NHL scouts as the fourth pick overall. He was aware that at least two teams were looking at him as a possible draft pick. Jimmy Devellano, general manager for the Detroit Red Wings, brought Steve to Detroit for a visit and let him know they were interested in him.

"He pretty much did most things well for a player of his age," Devellano remembers. "Certainly he could skate. He had good hockey sense. He could handle the puck. He was able to score and make plays. That's about all you want in a hockey player! And he was able to do those things above average for a kid his age."

But Devellano did not want to give Steve false hope. He told Steve he was looking to pick the highest-rated player available when his turn came. There was a good chance that could be Waterford, Michigan, native Pat LaFontaine, who was rated third.

"Certainly I was up front with Steve," says Devellano, now senior vice-president with the Wings. "You were dealing with two pretty good hockey players – Pat LaFontaine and Yzerman – probably fairly equal and both were 18. The advantage one had was he was Detroit born and bred. Obviously, that was an important consideration because in 1983, Detroit wasn't 'Hockeytown.' The building was three-quarters empty and selling tickets was very, very important."

Bill Torrey, general manager for the New York Islanders, had spoken with Steve on the phone. He also expressed an interest in Steve's talent. With his high rating, it looked certain he would be chosen early. He just didn't know by which team.

Steve didn't have a preference. He was just hoping to get picked. He thought about the chance to play for the Islanders. It was one of his favorite teams anchored by his favorite player, Bryan Trottier. But the Islanders also had won four consecutive Stanley Cups. Steve knew it would be difficult earning a position on a team full of such great talent.

Detroit, on the other hand, was in the process of rebuilding its team. Over the previous 17 seasons, the Red Wings made the playoffs only twice. Mike and Marian Ilitch of Little Caesars Pizza had purchased the team the previous summer. Devellano, the new general manager, had been the Islanders' chief scout for their first three Stanley Cup teams. He was hoping to work the same magic in Detroit. He wanted to start rebuilding the franchise with his first draft pick. Steve might earn a spot on the roster, but he would be playing for a struggling team.

"For me, getting drafted in Detroit was ideal because new management had taken over the year before and they really didn't have a lot of players under contract," Steve says. "They needed players. If I could keep up and I could play, I would have a job. I had a job to win or lose on my own. I was able to show that I could play at this level. It worked out well and I played regularly from the first game. For a young player, that's the

A familiar sight to Wings fans – Steve celebrates another goal.

ideal situation."

Bill Jamieson, director of public relations for the Wings from 1982-96, remembers this draft was important for Detroit. The Wings' fans were excited. It seemed everything businessman Mike Ilitch did was successful. They hoped he would have the same success with the floundering Wings.

"It was a big deal," says Jamieson. "It was the first draft of the Ilitch era. Anything Mr. Ilitch had been involved with, he'd had a real Midas touch. There was that same attitude toward the Red Wings. Now that Mike Ilitch owned the team, things were going to be better."

The day of the draft was exciting. Steve was nervous but, thanks to his high rating, he did not have to wait long to know his fate. The Minnesota North Stars nabbed Brian Lawton with the number one pick. Sylvain Turgeon, at number two, went to the Hartford Whalers. The New York Islanders drafted LaFontaine third. Moments later, Steve found out he would wear the winged wheel on his jersey, representing the Detroit Red Wings. He remembers the draft went quickly.

"It was a real whirlwind day," Steve says. "You get there and the draft starts. You're nervous. It's less pomp and circumstance than it is today. The guy steps up to the microphone and reads off the names and you go to the table. The Islanders picked third and chose Pat LaFontaine. I was picked by Detroit and went."

At Detroit's table, Steve met Mike and Marian Ilitch, Devellano, Jamieson, coach Nick Polano and some of the Detroit scouts. Jamieson whisked Steve off to do interviews by phone with the Detroit newspapers. It was the first of many times Steve would demonstrate his confidence and maturity for the Detroit media.

"He handled it well," remembers Jamieson. "He was just himself. He was very unpretentious."

Detroit started the 1983-84 season with high hopes. Prior to this, fans referred to the team as the "Dead Things." Since the mid-'60s, the Wings had managed to make the playoffs only twice, never going beyond the early rounds. Attendance was down. Consistent goal-scorers were nonexistent. That was about to change.

Steve made his NHL debut October 5, 1983, in a

road game against the Winnipeg Jets. He gave the Wings a quick return on their investment by scoring a goal and adding an assist. Still, the outcome was not in the Wings' favor. Detroit was leading 6-5 with only four minutes left in the game. Suddenly, the Jets' Doug Smail blazed in and put the puck past Wings goalie Eddie Mio. The game ended in a 6-6 tie, but Detroit's coaches saw what they wanted to see: a composed **rookie** who was ready to take on the NHL. In Bill McGraw's game story for the *Detroit Free Press* the next day, Coach Polano gave Steve high marks.

"He always looked dangerous," Polano said. "That tells you something, especially on the road. This was a good test for Steve. He showed he's ready to play."

Steve continued to show he was ready to play. In a 9-2 victory over the Toronto Maple Leafs on December 23, 1983, Steve got his first **hat trick**. He added an assist as the Wings ended an 11-game winless streak. For the rest of the season, Steve made a difference.

He posted 39 goals and 48 assists for a total of 87 points. This set team records for goals and points by a rookie. He was named top rookie by *The Sporting News* and voted to the NHL All-Rookie Team. Steve was runner-up in the voting for the Calder Trophy, which recognizes the NHL's Rookie of the Year. The Wings, who had been denied post-season play the previous five years, finished third and earned a playoff spot. In 1984, Steve was also picked to represent his country in the Canada Cup tournament. He returned to the Wings' training camp that fall with a gold medal as Canada beat Sweden. It was a great start, but only the beginning for a player who would become as recognized as the winged wheel on his jersey.

4

Hard Times in Hockeytown

Detroit is a tough sports town. The fans love their teams. At times, they also love to hate their teams. Especially when they are losing. Many years had passed since the Wings brought home four Stanley Cups in the 1950s. Detroit fans were getting hungry again. The 1984-85 season held promise as Steve scored 30 goals and had 59 assists. This gave him two points beyond his production as a rookie. The team finished third in the Norris Division but was ousted by the Chicago Blackhawks in the first round of the playoffs. Still, Steve was seen as a valuable asset to the team and on his way to becoming a star player.

The 1985-86 season was a disappointment. A little more than halfway through, Steve had tallied only 14 goals and 28 assists. For a player of his ability, it fell short of the mark. Then, in a game against St. Louis,

Steve fractured his collarbone. It was his first major injury and he missed the rest of the season. Coaching duties split between Harry Neale and Brad Park gave the Wings only 17 wins in 80 games. The Wings finished in last place, not even making the playoffs.

In an attempt to get the Wings back on their feet, the club hired coach Jacques Demers. Demers brought new enthusiasm to the job and capitalized on the Wings' assets. One of those assets was Steve, one of the strongest players on the roster. In a bold move, Demers named Steve his team captain at training camp that fall. At 21, he was the youngest captain in Red Wings history and in the NHL.

"It kind of caught me off guard," says Steve. "Jacques Demers was just named coach of the team. When he first came, he called me into his office and said, 'I want to name you captain. What do you think?' I was surprised. I didn't expect it. Looking back, it was good for me because it really made me reassess. I had come off a difficult year, a bad year. I'd gotten off to a poor start. Then, when I finally started playing better, I got injured and missed the last 30 games of the year.

"But becoming the captain really made me work a little bit harder. I came to practice every day with the attitude that I was going to get something out of it. [I thought] 'I'm going to practice hard and, in the games, I'm going to compete hard.' It really made me focus on hockey."

Demers' style brought about other changes in Steve's role on the team. Scoring goals and dishing out assists would be only two pieces of the puzzle.

"He's the one who really started to use me more in a role," says Steve. "I still played the offensive part of the game, but he started to use me for killing penalties and **face-offs**. Our team was expected to keep the goals against (**goals-against average**) down, and soon, we were all expected to play in both ends of the rink."

That season the Wings improved, finishing second in the Norris Division standings. Their record went from a miserable 17-57-6 to a more respectable 34-36-10. They made it all the way to the Campbell Conference finals, where they lost to the Edmonton Oilers, eventual

Face-offs are a key role in which Steve excels for the Wings. He takes one here against the New Jersey Devils.

winners of the Stanley Cup. Steve was the key to the Wings' playoff success, leading the team with five goals and 13 assists.

Things continued to look up as Steve entered the 1987-88 season. He dominated the scoreboard, getting 49 goals in the first 63 games. Then, as Cynthia Lambert of *The Detroit News* wrote, "The worst thing that could possibly happen to the Red Wings happened..."

During the second period of a 4-0 win over the Buffalo Sabres, March 1, 1988, Steve slid into the goalpost. He injured his right knee and ended his best regular season to date. Earlier in the period, Steve scored his 50th goal of the season. He set a club record by scoring 50 goals in fewer games than any other Red Wing. Steve also had an assist, giving him 102 points, 40 more than any teammate at the time. After being taken to Detroit's Hutzel Hospital, Steve was told he had severely strained his **posterior cruciate ligament**. Many people thought his season was over.

But Steve never doubted himself. Choosing not to have surgery on the knee, he worked hard to rehabilitate the muscles surrounding it. He worked out in the team's weight room twice a day.

"I never once thought I wouldn't be able to play

again," Steve remembers. "At the time, I was concerned that it may shorten my career. That was about all. I wasn't too worried about that one."

Steve kept himself occupied by continuing his daily workouts and, during the playoffs, writing columns for

Steve puts the puck past Chicago Blackhawks goalie Ed Belfour.

the *Detroit Free Press*. Although Steve was disappointed that he wasn't playing, he did get to share his thoughts and insights with fans as the Wings fought their way through the post-season.

The Wings made it to the Campbell Conference finals, once again facing the Edmonton Oilers. Edmonton won the first two games of the series on its home ice. The crowd in Detroit's Joe Louis Arena showed its appreciation with thunderous applause when Steve, The Captain, unexpectedly returned to the lineup for a 5-2 win in Game 3. But the Oilers would prevail. They beat Detroit the next two games and went on to win their fourth Stanley Cup in five years.

For two more years, Demers tried to make Detroit a champion. The Wings had greatly improved the first two seasons he coached. But in 1989 they lost in the first round of the playoffs and in 1990 failed to qualify, finishing last in the Norris Division. The next season the Wings hired coach Bryan Murray, who did not meet management's expectations. Although Detroit had drafted many players who offered more support to Steve on the ice, he continued to be the team's best player. Offensively, he carried the weight of the Detroit Red Wings on his back. From 1987-88 through 1992-93, Steve had more than 100 points every season, including career highs of 155 points and 65 goals in 1988-89, but it wasn't enough. The Wings continued to lose in the playoffs, always ending their season long before the Stanley Cup was hoisted into the air by another NHL team.

Still, a series of difficult, frustrating seasons seemed to be coming to a close. The Wings continued to build with players such as Sergei Fedorov, Nicklas Lidstrom and Ray Sheppard. Through it all, Steve remained a constant. He quietly went about the business of scoring goals and keeping Detroit in contention for the Cup. With consistent play, great composure, a number of club records and a rehabilitated knee, Steve had shown just what kind of player he was: a true hockey professional full of perseverance and determination. It was something hockey fans would see again and again as Steve continued his own quest for the Cup.

5

The Bowman Era

Over the years, Scotty Bowman earned the reputation of being a tough coach. By 1993, he had also earned seven Stanley Cup rings, six of those as a head coach. In 1991, he was inducted into the Hockey Hall of Fame.

Detroit had fared well in recent seasons but seemed to stumble when playoff time came. The club decided it was time for another coaching change. This time, it wanted a coach whose record showed he could finish the job. The Wings believed that coach was Scotty Bowman.

While Steve enjoyed many accomplishments in his 10 seasons as a Red Wing, he had yet to guide his team to a Stanley Cup win. For him, it was the only true measure of success. Years of falling short started to take a toll on the young captain. Perhaps Bowman's experience and Steve's determination would combine for that winning result.

Before Bowman's arrival, in 1993, Detroit acquired players who would set the stage for some serious runs at the Stanley Cup. Sergei Fedorov and Dino Ciccarelli added some offensive punch while Nicklas Lidstrom and Vladimir Konstantinov anchored the defense. Now, with Bowman taking over the team, expectations were high that the Wings would surpass the improvements made by Jacques Demers and Bryan Murray. Bowman admits he had a strong club the first year he coached in Detroit.

"They had a high-scoring team," Bowman remembers. "They had a lot of good, young players that were in their developmental years. I more or less wanted to get a defensive system in place and get the goals against down. Their offense was strong."

Bowman also realized he had a quality player when he watched Steve.

"He was a great talent," Bowman says. "You know, a strength is talent plus work ethic. They're the two components you have to have and he had both of them."

But Bowman didn't get to see the depth of Steve's talent that first year. Steve's contributions were once again minimized by injury. In a game against the Winnipeg Jets October 21, 1993, Steve was hit from behind by Thomas Steen and crashed into the boards. A **herniated disk** would cause Steve to miss 26 games. Unlike his previous injuries, Steve was concerned about this one.

"When I had the surgery on my neck, that one made me a little bit nervous," says Steve. "I thought, 'I am going to come back from this, but am I going to be a good player again? Am I going to be able to take a solid hit?' It took me a little bit longer to really feel comfortable after that injury."

John Wharton, athletic trainer for the Wings, was concerned too. He remembers the surgery as if it were yesterday.

"He herniated a disk on his **cervical spine**," Wharton recalls. "They took a two-inch chunk of bone from his hip and placed it where the disk would be. Following that you've got to be in a **halo** and pretty much immobilize the neck for two months. After that, it's a very grueling, strenuous program of strengthening the spine, increasing the range of motion and getting your function back. Real simple things, [such] as looking to the left or looking to the right while you're driving, were a chore for him."

Wharton says that Steve exceeded the expectations for recovery.

"The immobilization period, I think, was the toughest for him," Wharton says. "He's so used to being an active person. But true to Stevie's form with every injury he's had, he really worked hard. I think he was ready about two months before he would have normally been, if he was an average person. Once he gets the green light to strengthen and rehab, he does it as quick and as efficiently as anybody I have ever seen."

But Wharton also knows there were reasons for Steve's quick healing.

"Looking after yourself and having a high threshold for pain are two things that make you an excellent candidate to be a quick healer," Wharton says. "He really looks after his body. He eats the right things. He gets the right amount of rest. He knows his body very well so he can get by with the amount of pain he can tolerate for certain situations."

Back on the ice, Sergei Fedorov would take Steve's place as center on the Wings' number one line. He also took over the duties of captain. The new depth of the Red Wings started to show as the team went about winning without Steve's help. When he returned to the lineup, Steve was still a key player. In his 58 games that season, Steve scored 24 goals and added 58 assists for 82 points.

The Wings led all NHL teams in scoring with 356 goals during Bowman's first year behind the bench. They finished in first place and felt confident about their chances going into the playoffs. Even the fans felt confident when they realized Detroit's first-round opponent was the San Jose Sharks. The Sharks had been in the league only three years and were seeded eighth in the playoffs.

The Wings were surprised by the Sharks' tenacity. The series seesawed for the entire seven games. A 4-0 shutout by Wings goalie Chris Osgood in Game 2 and a 7-1 rout by the Wings in Game 6 could not provide enough momentum to carry the team. The Wings lost the series at home on April 30 as the Sharks beat them 3-2.

Stunned by an early loss to a supposedly inferior team, the Wings tried to regroup. Throughout the off-season, Detroit fans and media chastised the Wings' players and staff. Bowman was viewed as nothing more than an expensive replacement for men who had done the same mediocre job years before. Steve and his teammates were seen as overpaid, over-indulged players who couldn't get the job done.

June editions of Detroit newspapers were heavy with rumors of trading The Captain. The rumors also included a number of his teammates. Steve decided to sit back and let the trade talk take its course. The pain in his back and neck from the October collision with Steen had continued through the season. Ignoring the rumors, he focused on getting healthy and being ready to play that fall. It was the best thing he could have done. To ease the pain in his back and neck, surgery was scheduled that summer. It helped stop the rumors. None of the other teams would want to buy a player with that kind of injury. There would be three to five months of rehabilitation and no guarantee what he would be capable of afterward.

While Steve went through his rehabilitation, Bowman set out to create a new game plan for the next season. Associate coach Barry Smith, returning from a coaching stint in Sweden, suggested a defensive system, the "left wing lock", that European teams were using. Bowman and associate coach Dave Lewis agreed.

"It's a basic system where you have three guys back," says Lewis. "It's usually the **forward** back on the left side of the rink. You're trying to prevent an attack and, if you can, create turnovers in the **neutral zone**."

At training camp that fall, Steve listened to merits of the new strategy. It would mean making some changes in his playing style. Although individual statistics might fall, the Wings would have fewer goals scored against them. This would generate more wins. As always, Steve looked at the bigger picture. His statistics didn't matter. What mattered was winning the Stanley Cup. Putting the team first, Steve dedicated himself to playing and promoting the left wing lock. Coach Smith recognized the effort Steve put into applying this system.

"I think Stevie knows that to stay in this league and be a top performer, you have to play both ends," Smith says. "The game has changed now and the recognition goes to those players who play well defensively, not just offensively. He was able to work on his game. He had the skills to do it before, he just wasn't asked to do it."

Camp went well. The Wings were eager to start the season armed with their new weapon. However, NHL team owners had another idea. Fueled by the rise in players' salaries, many teams were experiencing financial problems. The players and owners could not agree on a contract. When the exhibition season ended, the owners created a lock of their own. For 103 days, teams were locked out and not allowed to play. After the sides came to an agreement, the NHL season started January 20, 1995. It was decided each team would play only 48 games, all against teams in the same conference.

Steve revisited Bowman's comments from training camp. He reviewed Dick Todd's philosophy at Peter-

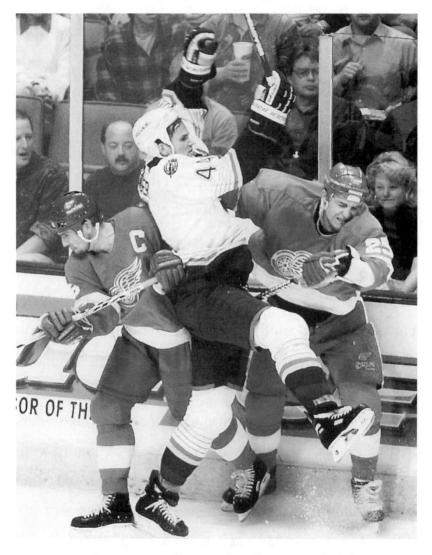

**Steve and teammate Darren McCarty sandwich
St. Louis Blues' defenseman Chris Pronger.**

borough. His game would become more defense ori-

ented. Individual statistics would be sacrificed for the

good of the team. Even better, the rest of the Red Wings stood by The Captain with the same belief. As difficult as it might be, Steve was ready to make that sacrifice.

"When Scotty came in, he totally changed it," Steve remembers. "It became, 'I don't care how many goals we get, if we get five goals or 50 goals, I better be able to count on you guys every game, defensively, every shift. You've got to be good defensively.' So the difficult part was to see your statistics come down. Everybody's saying, 'He's not the player he once was... time to trade him; get something while we still can. He doesn't score like he used to.' They want you to be a good defensive player, but you're not producing. You're doing what you're expected to do, what they (the coaches) want you to do."

At the end of the shortened season, the results of Bowman's strategies were obvious. The Wings won the Presidents' Trophy, awarded to the team with the NHL's best regular-season record (33 wins, 11 losses, 4 ties). They skated easily through the playoffs, ending the Dallas Stars' season in five games, the San Jose Sharks' in four, and the Chicago Blackhawks' in five. For the first time since 1966, the Detroit Red Wings were going to the Stanley Cup finals.

Steve finally saw his dreams becoming reality. The team had dominated through the regular season and the playoffs. The Wings were favored to win it all. Despite suffering a knee injury in the second round of the playoffs, Steve was playing and ready to take on the New Jersey Devils.

But it was not meant to be. The Wings were swept by the Devils in four games. Steve played well but not at the top of his game due to the injury. He scored only one goal in a series in which his team was outscored 16-7. With the rest of the Wings, Steve once again returned to Detroit greatly disappointed. His only hope, as before: next season.

6

The Fans Speak

The summer of 1995 was a long one. It was long for Scotty Bowman. He knew more changes had to be made. It was long for Steve Yzerman. He returned to the Wings' camp that season with an uncertain future.

Trade rumors surrounded Steve once again. His back and knee injuries were completely rehabilitated. He was a healthy center with solid statistics. There was no upcoming surgery, as there had been in 1994. Detroit could easily put Steve up for trade. The Senators, from his hometown of Ottawa, were seriously looking to acquire him. True to his style, Steve did not seek attention from teammates, management or the media by pleading his case to stay in Detroit. He quietly went about his job and resigned himself to the fact that this was business.

"Everybody handles things a different way," Steve says. "I know how this business works and you're going to go to a team that isn't going to win it in the next few years. The biggest reason I didn't want to be traded was I was going from one of the best teams in the league to wherever I was going to be traded. It wasn't going to be a good team. So my approach was 'I'm going to play. I'm going to play well. And whatever happens happens.'"

As the date of the Wings' home opener neared, Steve's status had not changed. Steve donned his Wings **sweater** October 13, 1995. At the pre-game ceremonies, the team was awarded banners for its previous season's accomplishments: the Presidents' Trophy, the Western Conference title and the Central Division title. As the banners rippled in the rafters of Joe Louis Arena, announcer Budd Lynch introduced the team. When he read, "Number 19… Steve Yzerman," the fans responded with a deafening ovation. They stood and chanted, "Stevie! Stevie! Stevie!" for well over a minute. Detroit fans had spoken. They wanted the Stanley Cup. They did not want to win it without their captain. Although Steve felt it was a nice gesture, he also knew fan support alone wouldn't keep him in Detroit.

"It was really nice," Steve says. "I appreciated it. But the reason I stayed is because I played well. If I hadn't played well, I would have been traded. I had to produce. I feel I did that."

Still, Scotty Bowman seemed to get the fans' message. The trade rumors ended and Detroit began a season of domination in the NHL. The Wings pummeled team after team, racking up a record-setting 62 wins in the regular season. They scored 325 goals to their opponents' 181. Steve scored 95 points (36 goals, 59 assists). Once again, the Wings were the team to beat. They were heavily favored to win the Cup as the playoffs started.

Round 1 was against the Winnipeg Jets. The Wings outscored the Jets 20-10 in the series. With all that offense, it still took Detroit six games to end the Jets' season.

St. Louis stretched the Wings even further in Round 2. The Wings opened the series with a confident 2-0 lead. They stifled Brett Hull and shut down Wayne Gretzky, leaving the Blues looking old and weary. Game 3 changed everything. An overtime win gave new life to the Blues. They went on to win the next two games, putting the series at 3-2. Facing elimination, the Wings mustered every ounce of energy they had left. They won a tough 4-2 decision, forcing a Game 7 back in Detroit. In the first six games, Steve scored four goals (three of those a **natural hat trick** in Game 3) and assisted on three others. But none of these points would compare to the one he was yet to get. It produced one of the most memorable moments of Steve's career.

The score remained 0-0 through three periods of regulation play and one period of overtime. Fans in Joe Louis Arena held their breath with every shot on goal. About a minute into the second overtime, Steve snatched the puck from Gretzky and, near the **blue line**, sent a **slap shot** whizzing past Blues goalie Jon Casey. The goal stunned Casey and the Blues. It also surprised The Captain.

"I shot it and looked up and heard the clang against the bar," Steve told *Detroit Free Press* reporter Viv Bernstein, "and I was like, 'No way. It went in!'"

The Wings' players mobbed their captain, celebrat-

Buried under a pile of happy teammates, the Wings celebrate Steve's game winning goal in double-overtime against St. Louis during the 1996 playoffs.

ing the 1-0 victory. They were heading to the Western Conference finals.

Steve and his teammates didn't have long to revel in the victory. Three days later, the Colorado Avalanche stormed into Joe Louis Arena. With incredible size and speed, the Avalanche quickly took a 2-0 lead in the series on Detroit's home ice. Detroit headed to Denver determined to show the Avalanche it would not roll over and die. The Wings came out shooting in Game 3, earning a 6-4 win. But Game 4 would put Detroit in an all too familiar situation. After a 4-2 loss, Detroit headed home facing elimination. The Wings fought back with a 5-2 victory. Did they have back-to-back wins in them? The team thought so. Detroit fans hoped so. Tension kept building as the series moved back to Colorado. Yet nothing could prepare the Wings or their fans for what was to come.

From the opening face-off, Game 6 had all the beginnings of a new NHL rivalry. The players battled. The

During the 1996 Game 6 loss to the Avs, a Colorado fan reminds Steve how long it has been since a Red Wing hoisted the Stanley Cup.

coaches, who had traded criticism in the news media, argued across the benches. This game would come to characterize all future meetings between the two teams. The event that pushed the rivalry front and center was Claude Lemieux's hit from behind on Wings center Kris Draper. Slammed into the boards face first, Draper suffered a series of facial fractures and a broken jaw. Even with the motivation of revenge for Draper, the Wings lost the game 4-1. Colorado went on to beat the Florida Panthers in a four-game sweep and hoist the Stanley Cup.

Once again, Steve's season ended short of his goal. He led his team in the playoffs, scoring eight goals and adding 12 assists. He scored his 500th goal, January 17, 1996, against Colorado during the regular season.

But that didn't matter.

Personal statistics never mattered.

What mattered was whether or not your team won the Stanley Cup.

Next season, Steve and his teammates would try again.

7

Lord Stanley's Cup

It had been 42 years since the Stanley Cup had called the city of Detroit home. After seeing the Cup within reach the two previous seasons, Steve and the Wings pushed even harder. The 1996-97 season would be different. It had to be.

During the off-season, Steve played for Team Canada in the World Cup of Hockey tournament. During the tournament, he was impressed by the play of fellow Canadian Brendan Shanahan. Shanahan was a power forward with a wicked shot. A couple of months later, Steve got the opportunity to play again with Shanahan. This time it was with the Wings. The day of their home opener, October 9, the Wings sent Keith Primeau and Paul Coffey, along with a number one draft pick, to the Hartford Whalers. In exchange, Shanahan arrived at Joe Louis Arena just as the Wings were about to head onto the ice for warm-ups.

"It was a whirlwind day," remembers Shanahan. "The Wings basically called me up and said, 'Go to the airport and we'll have our plane waiting there. The deal's not done yet but we hope it will be done by the time you land in Detroit. If not, we'll fly you home.'"

The Wings waited a few extra minutes for Shanahan to dress. Then, as a team, they all came onto the ice. Although he didn't score, he was a versatile left **wing** on the ice for power plays and penalty killing. His contributions helped Detroit beat the Oilers 2-0, stopping their three-game winning streak.

As the season rolled on, the Wings seemed to take everything in stride. Scotty Bowman seemed to switch his lines every game. No one argued. Each of the Wings went out on the ice every night and played the role he was asked to play, following Steve's example.

"One of the best things about playing hockey with Steve," Shanahan says, "is the fact that he shows up every night to play. You never have to worry about your linemate taking a night off. Every night he shows up to play his best."

Early in November, Steve signed a four-year contract. It compensated him as one of the Wings' top players, and assured him a place in Wings management when
his playing career ended. In February, Steve passed another milestone when he played his 1,000th NHL game.
As the season came to a close, Steve turned in another
respectable set of statistics with 22 goals and 63 assists
for 85 points.

Although the Wings seemed confident, they did not
dominate as they had previously in the regular season.
Their record was third best in the Western Conference
at 38-26-18. Perhaps the Wings had finally put the regular season in perspective. It was important to play well
and get a decent **playoff berth**. It was more important
for the team to turn up the intensity and narrow its focus
during the playoffs. Everything was falling into place.

Their first victim would be the St. Louis Blues. The
teams split the first two games in Detroit. In St. Louis,
Steve scored on the power play in Game 3 as the Wings
won 3-2. Blues goalie Grant Fuhr got his second shut-

out of the series in Game 4, but the Wings' 5-2 win in Game 5 put St. Louis one game from elimination. The Wings ended the series two nights later with a 3-1 win at Joe Louis Arena.

The second round brought the Anaheim Mighty Ducks. Games 1 and 2 combined for four periods of overtime but Detroit got the deciding goal in each. Down 2-0 in Game 3, the Wings rallied back to win 5-3. They finally swept the series in Game 4 with a 3-2 win in double overtime.

Round 3 brought back the rivalry everyone wanted to see. The Wings vs. Colorado, the defending Stanley Cup champion. While fans and the media played up the angle of revenge for Kris Draper, Steve remembers it was not the team's focus.

"We weren't talking about that," Steve says. "We weren't focused on Claude Lemieux. They had too many other players. We just wanted to beat Colorado. We wanted to win."

The Avalanche took advantage of home ice, winning 2-1 in the first game. Leading the comeback in

Game 2, Steve scored the game winner as the Wings won 4-2. The Wings won the next two games, shocking the Avs 6-0 in Game 4. But Colorado wasn't finished. Back home, the Avs got back into the series, repeating the 6-0 score.

Now it was Detroit's turn to make home ice an advantage. The Wings eliminated Colorado with a 3-1 victory. Steve accepted the Campbell Conference bowl, quickly acknowledged the crowd, and skated off the ice. It was another game won. The Wings had at least four more to go. It was time to take on the Philadelphia Flyers in the Stanley Cup finals.

The Flyers were a big, hard-hitting team. Detroit was ready for them. The Wings played smart and skated fast throughout Game 1. Detroit led 3-2 after two periods. Then, just 56 seconds into the third period, Steve wound up for a slap shot from the blue line, beating Flyers goalie Ron Hextall. Breaking with tradition, the Wings took Game 1 of the series, 4-2, in Philadelphia. The Wings had not won a game in the finals since April 26, 1966, when they beat the Montreal Canadiens for a

2-0 lead in the series. But those Wings had lost the Cup four games later. This was just the first of many traditions to be broken.

The Wings returned for a repeat performance in Philadelphia three nights later. The Flyers started goalie Garth Snow after Hextall's weak performance in Game 1. It didn't seem to matter. Steve put the Wings ahead early in the first period with a power-play goal. Shanahan scored two goals and Kirk Maltby added another as Detroit won 4-2. It was an enviable position. The Wings were heading back to Detroit with a 2-0 lead, knowing they could very well win the Stanley Cup at home.

Steve got the Wings' first goal of Game 3 on a power play. As the Wings racked up goals, the Detroit fans cheered every hit, pass or blocked shot by a player in red and white. When it was over, the scoreboard flashed a 6-1 Wings victory. Steve was one game away from his lifetime dream. But Bowman told reporters his team would have little time to enjoy the victory.

"We're three-fourths of the way there, that's the way I look at it," Bowman said. "I told the players to enjoy the win for five minutes, then start thinking about the next game."

And think they did. Nicklas Lidstrom slapped a shot

Steve and Wings celebrate Detroit's first Stanley Cup in 42 years. The Wings swept the Philadelphia Flyers in four games.

home in the first period of Game 4 for a 1-0 lead. In the second period, Darren McCarty faked out a **defenseman** and then Hextall, putting Detroit up 2-0. The score held well into the third period until Hextall, the Flyers' goalie, headed toward the bench to give Philadelphia another attacker. With 14.8 seconds left in the game, Eric Lindros scored his only goal of the series for the Flyers. It was too little, too late. Fifteen seconds later, the Wings were celebrating a 2-1 victory and a sweep of the Flyers.

NHL commissioner Gary Bettman met Steve at center ice. As the crowd cheered, he presented Steve with the Stanley Cup. Steve hoisted the Cup high and turned to his team to share the honor. But his teammates had a different idea.

"He had

Following Detroit's first Stanley Cup championship in 42 years, Steve (second from right) celebrates back home in Nepean with his sister Roni-Jean and brothers Gary and Christopher.

suffered so many defeats and had shouldered a lot of the responsibility in previous years," Shanahan recalls. "He turned to bring the Cup over to the team and we all pointed for him to take a lap himself because he had earned it. It was a great moment to be his teammate."

Steve started his skate around the rink. He looked for his parents and his wife in the stands. Part way around the ice, he stopped in front of Mike Ilitch, letting him raise the trophy high. After 14 long and often difficult years, Steve's dream had become a reality.

"I don't know how to describe how I feel," Steve told reporters. "I'm glad the game is over, but I wish it never ended."

Looking back, associate coach Dave Lewis, like all the members of the Wings organization, remembers how special it was seeing Steve with the Cup.

"A favorite Yzerman moment?" he asks. "It's when he held the Stanley Cup over his head. Prior to that season, Steve was criticized locally and nationally for not being a leader, not being able to lead his team to victory. He was taking a lot of unfair criticism. I was so happy to see him raise that Cup over his head."

Steve looked forward to a summer in which he would be in the very position he had seen Wayne Gretzky and Mario Lemieux enjoy. No one could take away the pride and feeling of accomplishment brought about by winning a Stanley Cup.

But the celebrations of Steve and his teammates *would* be cut short . . .

8

Back "TWO" Back

Less than a week after the Wings won the Stanley Cup, a tragedy befell them. Teammates Vladimir Konstantinov and Slava Fetisov and team **masseur** Sergei Mnatsakanov were returning home after a golf outing in Washington Township, Michigan, Friday, June 13, 1997. The driver of their limousine crashed into a tree, injuring all three men. By Sunday, Fetisov was listed in good condition while Konstantinov and Mnatsakanov remained critical. After only six days of celebrations and parades, Steve returned to his role as captain and spoke for all the Wings players at a hospital news conference.

"Our entire organization is devastated by the accident," Steve said to reporters. "We request that you respect the privacy of the families and members of the organization. The players feel it is not appropriate to give out interviews because we don't quite understand everything that's involved and we prefer to let the doctors answer all those questions. We ask everyone's support and prayers for our teammate, Vladdie, and trainer, Sergei."

That September, the Wings returned to training camp for the 1997-98 season. Many of the Wings told the media that the season would be dedicated to keeping the Stanley Cup in honor of their injured teammates. Throughout the season, the team's sweaters bore patches that honored Konstantinov and Mnatsakanov. It reminded all the Wings that, although it was great to win, other things in life mattered more.

"Every time I thought about it, it was very saddening," Steve said of the accident. "It really kept things in perspective after we won. It brought everybody back down to earth, not just the hockey players but the Red Wing fans as well. It was absolutely the most important thing to win the Cup. Then you realize, after this terrible accident, there are more important things than winning. If you can take anything out of that accident that helped us, it's that any time there was heat or pressure on us, we were comfortable. We had the accident to remind us, 'Don't make more out of this than it is. Go out and play and it's not life or death.'"

That philosophy remained in Steve's mind the entire season. As the Wings played through another admirable season, Steve continued to break records, pass milestones and take advantage of opportunities.

Less than a month into the season, Steve moved up the list of NHL all-time scorers. In a 4-3 win over the San Jose Sharks, Steve scored goal number 544. He was tied for 15th place with Montreal Canadiens great Maurice "Rocket" Richard.

A few weeks later, Steve found out he would play for Team Canada in the 1998 Winter Olympics. He went to Nagano, Japan, as the **assistant captain** for the team, excited about the opportunity to represent his country. It was an experience he hasn't forgotten.

"I loved the atmosphere there," says Steve. "You were mingling with athletes from all over the world, getting to see guys who had just won a gold medal. The games were tough and we had a difficult loss to the Czechs, but it was a great experience."

Many of the Canadian hockey players brought their

Steve fights off the Washington Capitals' Sergei Gonchar during the 1998 Stanley Cup Finals.

families to Japan. They took in tourist attractions and spent time shopping. However, Steve's wife, Lisa, was home awaiting the birth of their second child. Although Steve took his Olympic ice time seriously, he also tried to find ways to have fun away from the rink. He and teammate Brendan Shanahan found one way. They were known for raiding the Olympic Village cafeteria for ice cream late at night.

"There wasn't a whole lot to do around there at night," Steve chuckles. "The food at the cafeteria was from all over the world; they had to please everybody, a little bit of everything. So we'd hang out and go there around 10 o'clock. Ice cream seemed like a good bedtime snack!"

"It was fun to go down to the cafeteria," Shanahan says. "You would see some athletes coming back late from competition." But as for the ice cream? "It was pretty basic – a scoop of vanilla. It was the only choice you had."

But beating the Czech Republic would prove to be much more difficult than finding flavors of ice cream. Team Canada would bow out in the semifinals, losing to the Czechs 2-1. Steve had a goal and an assist in six Olympic games. These games were the spark that fueled a flame. When Steve returned to Detroit, he began to focus on finishing the NHL season with another Stanley Cup. The mid-winter break seemed to be just what he needed. By the end of March, Steve led the Wings with 61 points. In a game against the Chicago Blackhawks, with the Wings down by three goals, Steve scored two goals and added two assists. The 5-5 tie clinched a playoff spot for the Wings. In the next game, Steve got his $1,400^{th}$ career point and 561st goal, passing Guy Lafleur for 12th place in goals. The Wings finished the season 44-23-15, second to Dallas in the Central Division and Western Conference.

In playoffs, the Wings beat Phoenix, St. Louis and finally Dallas to secure another spot in the Stanley Cup finals. Once again, the Wings showed their depth and determination, sweeping the Washington Capitals in four games. Steve raised the Stanley Cup and the Conn Smythe Trophy, which recognized him as the playoffs' Most Valuable Player. Even with the individual recognition, Steve felt it was winning that second Stanley Cup that validated his long career.

"The most important accomplishment is playing on

Voted Most Valuable Player of the 1998 playoffs, Steve
is awarded the Conn Smythe Trophy.

two Stanley Cup winners," Steve says. "That, to me, makes everything else insignificant. The fact that I was able to play on a team that's won two Cups and it's been the same organization that I have been with my whole career makes it more meaningful. I've put in a lot of time and effort to be a part of it, to be part of the team growing to be a *successful* team."

And so the parades and celebrations honoring Steve and his champion teammates started again. This time, they would last all summer.

9

The Road Ahead

It has been two seasons since the Wings won the Stanley Cup. Steve and the Wings made the playoffs both seasons, but they lost in the second round. Steve continues to be the Wings' top center. He also continues to lead as their captain in his quiet and unassuming way. His years in the NHL give him strengths that go beyond the basics of goal scoring or defense.

"I understand the game," Steve says. "I can adapt. I see a situation and do what I need to do."

But ask opponents what makes Steve a threat and they will tell you much more. Colorado Avalanche assistant coach Bryan Trottier has seen firsthand the damage Steve can do. Although Steve idolized him as a youngster, it's clear Trottier feels Steve has excelled well beyond Trottier's accomplishments as an NHL superstar.

"Steve surpasses me in puck control and stick handling," Trottier says. "He has a much better shot than I ever had, in accuracy and power. He has prided himself in his defensive game, for example face-offs, positioning and blocking shots, as well as back-checking."

As a coach, Trottier sees Steve as a tough opponent for a number of reasons.

"He is almost impossible to contain," Trottier says. "He can hurt you with his scoring or passing and he'll burn a defenseman with his stick handling. He wins so many face-offs, his team has the puck most of the night. His competitive drive and proud play will not allow him to give up. He works for 60 minutes, which makes him one of the great leaders of all time. As a fan and a coach, I see a gifted competitive athlete with skills of the highest level in every fundamental aspect of the game."

Darren Pang, his friend and former teammate in Nepean, agrees that Steve's hard work has helped put him in the NHL's elite.

"Watch how often after practice he stays out there and is one of the last guys to leave the ice," Pang says.

"He's working on face-offs, working on shooting, and working on **deking**. That's one thing that really stands out to me. It's the pride he takes in his work ethic. Then, when he gets on the ice, I would say he's currently one of the very best face-off men that there is in the game. He is, in my opinion, the best shot-blocking forward in the NHL. And besides, he's got the uncanny ability to just score big goals."

Jimmy Devellano agrees that Steve is one of a kind.

"I think he was the most important pick we made," Devellano says, looking back. "It was my first draft and we had an awful hockey team. The players we would draft in 1983 were hopefully going to be the building blocks for the future of the team. As it turns out, taking Yzerman fourth overall… he certainly became more than a building block. He became the pillar that the franchise was built around. Sometimes it pays to be lucky."

Although Steve is probably best known for his hard work on the ice, he is just as dedicated in his off-ice pursuits. Throughout his years in Detroit, Steve has been involved with a number of local charities. He has donated his time at hockey camps and, though not well publicized, he has been a frequent visitor to children in area hospitals.

"I've gotten to know a few of them quite well," he says. "Some have had battles with cancer, and beat it, fortunately. A couple of the kids I got involved with unfortunately passed away because of their illness."

But Steve views the situation positively.

"It's been especially rewarding for me because you have some influence on the kid and brighten their day a little bit," he says. "I have gotten to see how some of these kids deal with their problems. It's remarkable how tough they are. They deal with the adversity much better than some of the adults, myself included. We have problems far less than what they face."

Steve's family is also important to him. He lives in suburban Detroit with his wife, Lisa, and their three daughters, Isabella, Maria and Sophia. Steve feels making time for his family is not only a priority, it actually helps his hockey playing.

"I enjoy being home," Steve says. "There are two

Steve is recognized during a pre-game ceremony at Joe Louis Arena for scoring his 500th goal during the 1995-96 season. His wife Lisa and daughter Isabella join him.

things right now: my family and hockey. I just go to the rink and practice or play and then I come home. When you're struggling or your team's not playing well, you really have a tendency to over-think and get so wrapped up in it that it just doesn't help you at all. Having a family gives me the chance to forget about it and come to the rink really fresh the next day."

Although his family and hockey take up most of his time, Steve squeezes in a few other favorite activities. He's an avid golfer and likes to do crossword puzzles. He also enjoys boating and hitting the waves on a Sea-Doo when spending time at his summer cottage north of Toronto. He and Lisa also enjoy going to movies.

At age 35, Steve continues to put the finishing touches on his Hall of Fame career in Detroit. During the 1999-2000 season, Steve scored 35 goals and had 44 assists for 79 points. One of those goals, scored November 26, 1999, against Edmonton, was his 600th. An assist in a game November 17, 1999, against Vancouver was his 900th. He was awarded the Frank J. Selke Trophy as the NHL's best defensive forward. He carries on a captaincy that has reigned well over 1,000 games and 14 seasons. But Steve also realizes he can't play hockey, or be the captain, forever.

"I think in the near future it will be time for another

guy to come in and be the captain of the team," Steve says. "As some of the younger guys on our team mature, they're kind of taking over and they become the voice of, or the pulse of, the team. My group is becoming older now. I'm more of a veteran and my role is going to slowly decrease."

But many people believe Steve is playing some of the best hockey of his career. They wonder what else Steve will add to his stellar list of achievements. He has set team and league records, won individual awards, has made nine All-Star appearances, represented his country in international competition, and had his name inscribed on the Stanley Cup twice. He continues to amaze hockey fans and inspire his teammates and coaches.

"He's definitely the epitome of the guy who goes out and leads by example," says teammate Darren McCarty. "He's one of the hardest working guys, not only on the ice but off the ice too. He does all the little things that need to be done."

Steve also sets a great example for younger players on the team.

"He has shown me that, through all his greatness and all the records, it's still the same guy that you would know if he didn't have all the records," says Mathieu Dandenault, a Wing for six seasons. "It doesn't get to his head. He takes it all in stride. It's amazing to watch, the point in his career where he's done everything, and he just keeps working at it, working hard to be better."

John Wharton, the Wings' trainer, agrees that Steve sets a good example. He never stops working to be the best.

"He's an elite athlete when it comes to conditioning and training," Wharton says. "It's great to have your captain in such good shape and with such a good work ethic because it filters down throughout the rest of the team. The younger guys come in and see the effort that Steve's putting out. He leads by example, on the ice and in the weight room."

Associate coach Dave Lewis offers similar praise.

"Every team would love to have a player like Steve Yzerman on their team and every coach would love to coach him," says Lewis. "That's a tribute to him and one of the greatest compliments you can give a player."

In January 1999, the Nepean Raiders honored Steve by renaming their home rink *The Steve Yzerman Arena*. The last contract he signed in Detroit made him a Red Wing for life, including a front office position once his playing career is over.

"I think I would like to be a general manager," Steve says. "I want to scout and help build a team. I like to follow players and the trades made and see if I can fig-ure out why they did certain things. I enjoy picking out traits, seeing the building blocks that a player has."

Surely the Wings organization hopes that if he takes on that role, he can find them a player who will some-how compensate for the huge hole left in their roster. Number 19's skates will be difficult to fill.

Steve takes his good friend "Stanley" for a ride on his Sea-Doo.

Regular Season Statistics

Season	Team	League	Games Played	Goals	Assists	Points	Penalty Minutes
1981-82	Peterborough	OHL	58	21	43	64	65
1982-83	Peterborough	OHL	56	42	49	91	33
	Canada	**WJC-A**	7	2	3	5	2
1983-84	Detroit	NHL	80	39	48	87	33
1984-85	Canada	C Cup	4	0	0	0	0
	Detroit	NHL	80	30	59	89	58
	Canada	**WEC-A**	10	3	4	7	6
1985-86	Detroit	NHL	51	14	28	42	16
1986-87	Detroit	NHL	80	31	59	90	43
1987-88	Detroit	NHL	64	50	52	102	44
1988-89	Detroit	NHL	80	65	90	155	61
	Canada	WEC-A	8	5	7	12	2
1989-90	Detroit	NHL	79	62	65	127	79
	Canada	WEC-A	10	10	10	20	8
1990-91	Detroit	NHL	80	51	57	108	34
1991-92	Detroit	NHL	79	45	58	103	64
1992-93	Detroit	NHL	84	58	79	137	44
1993-94	Detroit	NHL	58	24	58	82	36
1995	Detroit	NHL	47	12	26	38	40
1995-96	Detroit	NHL	80	36	59	95	64
1996-97	Canada	W Cup	6	2	1	3	0
	Detroit	NHL	81	22	63	85	78
1997-98	Detroit	NHL	75	24	45	69	46
	Canada	Olympic	6	1	1	2	10
1998-99	Detroit	NHL	80	29	45	74	42
1999-00	Detroit	NHL	78	35	44	79	34

Playoff Statistics

Season	Team	League	Games Played	Goals	Assists	Points	Penalty Minutes
1981-82	Peterborough	OHL	6	0	1	1	16
1982-83	Peterborough	OHL	4	1	4	5	0
	Canada	WJC-A	-	-	-	-	-
1983-84	Detroit	NHL	4	3	3	6	0
1984-85	Canada	C Cup	-	-	-	-	-
	Detroit	NHL	3	2	1	3	2
	Canada	WEC-A	-	-	-	-	-
1985-86	Detroit	NHL	-	-	-	-	-
1986-87	Detroit	NHL	16	5	13	18	8
1987-88	Detroit	NHL	3	1	3	4	6
1988-89	Detroit	NHL	6	5	5	10	2
	Canada	WEC-A	-	-	-	-	-
1989-90	Detroit	NHL	-	-	-	-	-
	Canada	WEC-A	-	-	-	-	-
1990-91	Detroit	NHL	7	3	3	6	4
1991-92	Detroit	NHL	11	3	5	8	12
1992-93	Detroit	NHL	7	4	3	7	4
1993-94	Detroit	NHL	3	1	3	4	0
1995	Detroit	NHL	15	4	8	12	0
1995-96	Detroit	NHL	18	8	12	20	4
1996-97	Canada	W Cup	-	-	-	-	-
	Detroit	NHL	20	7	6	13	4
1997-98	Detroit	NHL	22	6	18	24	22
	Canada	Olympic	-	-	-	-	-
1998-99	Detroit	NHL	10	9	4	13	0
1999-00	Detroit	NHL	8	0	4	4	0

NHL Career Awards and Accomplishments through 1999-2000 Season

- Scored a goal and an assist in NHL debut vs. Winnipeg (10-5-83)
- Reached 50-goal mark in fewer games (55) than any other Red Wing (1988-89)
- NHL All-Rookie Team (1984)
- Voted top rookie by *The Sporting News* (1984)
- Runner-up for 1983-84 Calder Trophy (NHL Rookie of the Year)
- First wore captain's "C" in 1986-87 at the age of 21, youngest in Wings history
- Longest serving captain in NHL history in terms of games and seasons
- Two club-record nine-game goal streaks, 12 goals, 11/18/88 through 12/5/88, and 14 goals, 1/29/92 through 2/12/92
- Club-record 28-game scoring streak, 29 goals, 36 assists, 11/1/88 through 1/4/89
- 1988-89 Lester B. Pearson Award as top performer by vote of NHL Players Association
- Recorded 1,000[th] point with an assist at Buffalo 2/24/93
- 18 regular-season hat tricks (most recent at Chicago 2/14/93); tied with Gordie Howe for club record

- Three natural hat tricks (most recent at Toronto 11/17/90)
- 1,300th point with goal at Chicago 1/5/97
- Had three assists in 1,000th career game, vs. Calgary 2/19/97
- 800th career assist was a game-winning assist vs. Buffalo 3/28/97
- Scored 1,400th career point on a power-play goal vs. Buffalo 3/29/98
- Represented Team Canada as assistant captain in 1998 Nagano Winter Olympics
- In 1998 Stanley Cup playoffs, led all NHL players with 24 points (6-18-24) in 22 games
- Awarded the Conn Smythe Trophy as playoff MVP (1998)
- Two Stanley Cup championships (1996-97, 1997-98)
- Recorded 900th career NHL assist 11/17/99 at Vancouver
- Recorded 1,500th career NHL point 11/20/99 at Edmonton
- Played in 1,200th career NHL game 11/24/99 at St. Louis

- Became 11th player in NHL history to score 600 goals 11/26/99 vs. Edmonton
- In NHL records, ranked 6th (tied with Mark Messier) in all-time goals (627), eighth in all-time assists (935) and 6th in all-time points (1,562) entering 2000-2001 season
- Yzerman had 627 goals in 1,256 games while Messier had 627 goals in 1,479 games
- 935 assists as a Red Wing is second only to Gordie Howe (1,023)
- Has led team in points 11 times, goals six times and assists 10 times
- Topped 100-point mark six times (one of 13 in NHL history to do it six times in a row)
- Scored 50 goals or more five times
- Scored 60 goals or more twice
- Club-record 49 shorthanded goals
- 10 All-Star Game selections (1984, '88-93, '97, '99, 2000) Did not play in 1999 All-Star Game due to injury
- Won the Frank J. Selke Trophy for Best Defensive Forward (1999-2000)

Glossary

assistant captain (also known as **alternate captain**) A player who may question the referees for his team while on the ice. A team appoints a captain and up to two assistant captains so one of these players can be on the ice at all times.

back-checking to hinder an opponent who is trying to reach his attacking zone.

blue line the two blue lines divide a hockey rink into three sections: a team's defending zone, the neutral zone, and the team's attacking zone.

bobskates skates with double blades on the bottom. Used by beginning skaters to improve their stability and balance.

center the center player in the forward, or attacking, line.

CJHL Central Junior Hockey
League.

cervical spine The spine is made up of 33
bones. The top seven bones
in the neck make up the cervical spine.

defenseman one of two players who play
in or near the defensive zone
to assist the goalkeeper.

deke/deking a faking motion made by a
player carrying the puck.

face-off To start play at any time, the
puck is dropped between
two opposing players facing
each other.

forward a member of the attacking line. The center, left wing and right wing are all forwards.

goals-against average the average number of goals scored against a goalkeeper in a game.

halo a rigid, molded plastic frame used to immobilize the head and neck after injury. It sits on the shoulders supporting the chin and back of the head, extending up around the skull. It keeps the person from moving the neck in any direction while the injury is healing.

hat trick when one player scores three goals in a game.

herniated disk Between each bone of the spine is a disk. Disks are like small water balloons that absorb shock. When a disk is herniated, or injured, the inside bulges out, pressing on the spinal nerves, causing pain.

house leagues teams made up of players who have not reached the level of play to earn spots on travel hockey teams. These players play in local games at their home arenas.

masseur a man whose work is massaging athletes as part of their training and fitness program.

natural hat trick when three goals are scored consecutively by the same player in the same game.

neutral zone the center ice area between the two blue lines. It is called the neutral zone because it is neither an attacking zone nor a defensive zone.

NHL National Hockey League. The league started in 1917 and currently has 30 teams.

NHL Entry Draft originally known as the NHL Amateur Draft. Players register with the NHL and if eligible, are placed on the availability list by the NHL Central Registry. Eligible players can then be selected to play for a team.

playoff berth Of the 30 teams in the NHL,

eight in each conference are awarded the chance to participate in the first round of the playoffs based on their regular season records.

posterior cruciate ligament One of the main ligaments of the knee, it holds two bones together, the tibia (shin bone) and the femur (thigh bone).

protected list a list of players who will be kept by a team. These players cannot be drafted to play for another team.

rookie an athlete playing his/her first year in a professional sport.

slap shot when a player takes his stick back and then quickly swings it forward, firing the puck toward the goal.

Stanley Cup presented in 1893 by the Governor-General of Canada, Lord Stanley, as a trophy for the amateur hockey champions of Canada. Since 1910, it has recognized the champions of North America. Since 1926, only NHL teams have competed for it.

sweater team shirt or jersey. In the early days of hockey, team shirts were sweaters made out of wool.

WEC-A World & European Championship, Pool A. The top group of countries in the world (known as Pool A) compete for the World

Championship. The countries that make up the other pools (Pool B, Pool C and Pool D) play to qualify for promotion to the World Championship.

WJC-A   World Junior Championship, Pool A. This championship is similar to the World Championship, Pool A. The players compete in two age categories, under 20 or under 18.

wing or **winger**   a player who plays on either side of the center in the forward, or attacking, line.

Time Line

1965 Steve Yzerman is born on May 9 in Cranbrook, British Columbia.

1970 Attends his first hockey camp and joins his first organized team.

1975-81 Yzerman family moves to the Ottawa suburb of Nepean, Ontario. Steve plays two years of Junior A Tier 2 hockey in the Central Junior Hockey League for the Nepean Raiders.

1981-83 Drafted and plays with the Peterborough Petes of the Ontario Hockey League. He plays for Team Canada in the World Junior Championships. Steve is selected fourth pick overall by the Detroit Red Wings in the 1983 NHL Entry Draft in Montreal.

1984 Ends his rookie season with the Wings as runner-up for the Calder Trophy (NHL's Rookie of the Year), a member of the NHL All-Rookie Team and voted top rookie by *The Sporting News*.

1986 Named captain at 21, youngest in Wings' history.

1987-93 Has six consecutive 100 point seasons, including career high 155 points and 65 goals for the 1988-89 season.

1997 Detroit Red Wings win Stanley Cup in four games over the Philadelphia Flyers; it is the team's first championship in 42 years.

1998 Represents Canada on Olympic team in Nagano. Wings win Stanley Cup second consecutive year in four games over the Washington Capitals; Yzerman awarded Conn Smythe Trophy as playoffs' Most Valuable Player.

1999 Signs contract that will make him a Detroit Red Wing for the remainder of his career.

Index

Further Reading

Fitzgerald, Francis J., editor. *Steve Yzerman: Heart of a Champion*. Louisville, Kentucky: Adcraft Sports Marketing Inc., 1996.

Harris, Paul. *Steve Yzerman: The Quiet Captain*. St. Louis, Missouri: GHB Publishers, 2000.

Resources

A to Z Encyclopedia of Ice Hockey.
    www.azhockey.com

The Official Site of the National Hockey League.
    www.nhl.com

Detroit Red Wings Official Team Site.
    www.detroitredwings.com

Detroit Free Press.
    www.freep.com

Photo Credits

About the Author

Shelley Lazarus is an elementary Media Specialist and an avid sports fan. She resides in Royal Oak, Michigan, with her husband and two daughters.